The Exchange
Him for You

*A Short Guidebook of Preparation
for the Life to Come*

Stacie Shukanes

authorHOUSE®

AuthorHouse™
1663 Liberty Drive, Suite 200
Bloomington, IN 47403
www.authorhouse.com
Phone: 1-800-839-8640

First published by AuthorHouse 11/13/2008

ISBN: 978-1-4389-2882-1 (sc)
ISBN: 978-1-4389-2883-8 (hc)

Printed in the United States of America
Bloomington, Indiana

This book is printed on acid-free paper.

Dedication

To Leslie, my dearest and most precious daughter, you are the reason my Christianity started to bloom years ago, and I thank God everyday for the love and joy you have brought to me since the moment of your birth. This book is for you and your family—that they may come to believe. I love you all and pray God's blessings upon you!

Acknowledgements

There are many people whom I so dearly love who have been a vital part of inspiring me to write this book. Nadine, my "substitute" mother, as you like to call yourself, you are my mentor, my friend. I love you with all of my heart. Ed and Roxy, you two have been the greatest friends, and I thank you for being there for me through thick and thin. You know how much I love you both. Kay and Roger—I cherish and love you two, and I am so thankful and blessed that our paths crossed again, Kay. Sherry, Jackie, Mary and Marcie, you have all given me such encouragement that there are no words to express my gratitude. Toni, I thank you for plugging me in to Precept Upon Precept so many years ago and I miss you every time I go to class.

Marla and Harriet, you both inspire me to heavenly heights, and I savor our time together.

Most importantly, I give all the glory to God Almighty who is my strength and my comfort!

Contents

Introduction

The Exchange
Him for You

This is a conventional approach to something so serious that your life depends on it. This is the condensed version of life to death for man on earth as we know it, and it could be the most important book you will ever read.

What would I want to know if I missed the chance to know that there is a God out there—that He has always been there, but I was too stubborn, proud and caught-up in myself to believe that He could even exist? Notice how I put all of that in the past tense. But, it's actually not too late—yet. I want to make the following information so compelling that you will want to question what you thought you knew, not only about God, but about the hereafter and what He was actually *here after.* I intend to fill in these gaps that may seem small and unimportant, or even foolish to many of you. There could be areas of concern about the mysteries of God that you may be too apprehensive to ask a believer about because it's something you should have learned as a child, and now you think you're too old to question. I want to bring to your attention a clearer perspective about why any of us are here and why your life even matters. I also want you to have a quick reference through this book should I not be here to ask and you've waited too long to get serious about the future. After all, I could die tomorrow. I just hope I can get this written in time to plant some seeds in some of you; the rest is up to you and God. If I were you, an unbeliever, or even a doubter, I would want an easy read—we'll call it a "coffee table book"—that spells out the truths that will someday make sense when you see an account of your life.

I am going to quote some Scripture, not a lot, but enough to substantiate my claims. In this day and time, attention spans are short! This is not a "preachy book" that takes on a theme of "fire and brimstone," but it is serious enough for careful consideration of the choices you make as a human being.

I am in no way an authority on God's Word, but I have studied it with great enthusiasm for the last 15 years. God has led me in this endeavor because He has a plan for redemption that He wants you to understand. Unfortunately for many of my friends, they don't think they need this plan. **You know who you are.** You should also know how much you mean to me. Don't miss this chance!

For me, this book exemplifies the most reverent attempt to tell God's message. This has been the greatest privilege of my life to pass on to you what I have learned. The last thing I would ever want to do is misrepresent Him. I think that is why I was a lukewarm Christian for many years. The responsibility of learning His Word was so great. I just didn't want to mess it up and interpret the Bible from my perspective and not His. I finally stepped out there and jumped in with my whole mind and heart. What an experience it has been through that commitment to know Him through His Word!

Consider this an outline of "God" facts that can change the direction of your life. And, if it doesn't change the direction of your life now, at least you can look back through this book later, and hopefully it's not too late, and understand more clearly where this path could lead you when you come to that crossroad. When you have finally come to the place where you yourself are not enough—there has to be more than this life and me, myself and I—there is. It's God and He's huge.

Though this is a short book, it is my hope that you would be so overwhelmed by its message that you would want to delve into the Bible where the real transformation takes place—in a person's mind and heart. It's all in there—love, faith, joy, morality, murder, marriage, divorce, child rearing, psychology, history, architecture, farming, homosexuality, evil, life, death. It is the guidebook to life.

I have heard it said derogatorily that the Bible is a moral masterpiece used by man to keep mankind "in line" so to speak through the ages, a book not touched by the likes of any god, but man alone. In my own estimation, no human being could ever conceive of the intricacy woven through the Bible that links every book within It to form the whole, without Almighty God there to orchestrate It. You only have to read It to understand the measure of Its majesty, wisdom and grace that is of God. It is truth because It is God's written and inspired Word. You cannot read It and not be changed. It is not with arrogance that I tell you any of this, but it is with the hope that you, too, can share in the knowledge and love of God that is yours to receive.

Is your name in the Book of Life that Jesus speaks of or will there be no evidence that you ever even existed? I hope not, as does He.

I.
God

The Evidence

First of all, there is a God, and you are not He. It is difficult for us to reason in our own minds how small we really are and how infinitely huge He is because let's face it; it's all about us. Right? The comparison is staggering and yet, we try to imagine that we are on His level. We're not because HE IS MASSIVE!

There is a DVD I watched recently called *Indescribable* that made me question everything I thought I knew about God. I thought about if for days, not because it called into question my faith in Him, but because I had no idea He could be this big, this mighty, this—well—*indescribable*. This DVD shows the universe through the most elaborate photography I have ever seen, downloaded through the Hubble Space Telescope that NASA has processed and released for our amazement. The universe extends so far that we cannot even capture its entirety on film. Earth is like a spec of a spec of a spec of dust in a gnat's eyebrow by comparison. There is this organization of the galaxies and planets that is beyond comprehension. Our solar system can be likened to the size of a quarter as compared to the Milky Way Galaxy, likened to the North American Continent! We just keep building bigger telescopes hoping we're going to see it all, but our technology just can't get the whole picture. What we see is only a tiny fraction of God's neighborhood, much less His world. Just imagine what the "unseen" must be like in its size and scope if the "seen" is this big!

A very dear friend of mine, Marla Tokatly, shared the following information with me when I was just beginning my book, so I found its content most pertinent to the point I'm trying to make here. A Russian scientist visiting an American university said, "Either there is a God or there isn't. Both possibilities are frightening!" This is so true. If there is a God, we need to find out who he is and what he wants. If there is no God, we are in trouble. We are hurtling through space at 66,000 mph and no one is in charge. What a frightening thought! (Ray Comfort)

Then there are us, humans—so small, as the lens narrows, that we are almost undetectable in the "big" picture. Yet, just think of the intricacy of the human body. We are miracles by any stretch of the imagination. Some people certainly bought into the evolution theory, but honestly, where are those apes that are evolving into humans today? We have records that span thousands of years and yet, I've never seen any evidence of this transformation that we can identify within the timeframe of recorded history. Shouldn't there be some mutation that we could measure as the first stage of evolution from an ape today to a human being a thousand years from now? We could see that ape and say," Oh, look, there is Al, the ape, on his way to becoming one of us." There certainly have been changes through evolution in adapting plants, animals, and humans to their environmental circumstances, but I'm not convinced that we evolved from a primate, much less a fish, much less an amoeba, but then again—God can do anything!

I just cannot deny that there is a God who created all of this, me included. I cannot look around me and not see God everywhere. No, I've never "seen Him" seen Him, but the evidence of Him is in everything. Just the fact that I can *see* anything is a miracle. Think about the eyeball—so amazing in its construction and function. The technology of the eye surpasses anything that any human could ever conceive of. Can you really think that someone far more intelligent than us didn't come up with that design or do you honestly believe it just "banged" into existence? Wow, now for me, that is a real reach! Just the essence of life in all of its complexity has order and pattern that cannot have been created without a Creator.

It seems so contrary to nature that we would exist on this earth without a purpose or a reason for living—we just live, die and we're done! Or, do those of us who believe there is something more than this, go on to something more than this?

The Godhead

*I*t is a great mystery—The Godhead, but it of course makes perfect sense when it's understood. The Godhead is based on Scriptural truth. There is one God who is made up of 3 divine persons—the Father, the Son and the Holy Spirit. "For there are three that bear record in heaven, the Father, the Son and the Holy Ghost, and these Three are One" (I John 5:7). This relationship is unique and beyond our human understanding, but it is a truth that by faith, is revealed to those of us who believe. The plan for redemption involves all three members. It was conceived by the Father, salvation is delivered through the Son, Jesus Christ, and the Holy Spirit abides in us as the communicating truth and force of God.

When you look at your own person, you exist in much the same way—1) you have a mind where you formulate thoughts, 2) you have a body made of flesh, bone and blood that everyone sees, and 3) you have a spirit that is your essence or soul. It was described to me this way some years ago—I cannot remember by whom—when I was struggling with the concept of the Godhead: my leg or arm is part of me, but it does not have much to do with how or what I think or my level of intelligence. My thoughts are not my spirit either. I may be upset about something and it is my spirit or emotions, not my flesh or mind, that is affected. In Matthew 26:41, Jesus gives further meaning to this, "The Spirit is willing, but the body is weak," as He spoke to His disciples trying to keep them awake to pray before He was betrayed and arrested in the Garden of Gethsemane.

So, to summarize, Jesus is in subjection to the Father, just as my arm or leg is in subjection to my mind. My mind has to tell my arm to move in order for movement to take place. That doesn't change the fact that my arm is still part of me. God sent Jesus to this earth for one primary reason—to save you and me—it is this plan that the entire Godhead is responsible for.

Jesus

I want to expand a little further about the person of Jesus Christ before we move on to other topics because belief in Him is the most important thing you will ever know on this earth.

He fulfilled the Scriptures exactly as God said, down to the most infinitesimal detail. In a class I took from Beth Moore called *Living Beyond Yourself,* she referenced the following information that is positively amazing about the prophecy of Jesus. From the journal, *Science Speaks,* Peter Stoner stated the following calculations about this fulfillment: if you take only 8 prophesies out of 61 that were foretold by God, the probability of all 8 being fulfilled is 1 in 10 to the 17th power. He illustrates it this way: take 10 to the 17th (or 100,000,000,000,000,000) silver dollars and lay them on the face of Texas. They will cover all of the state two feet deep. Now mark one of these silver dollars and stir up the coins. Blindfold a man and send him out to pick up the marked silver dollar. The chance that he will pick up the right one is 1 in 10 to the 17th power. If we add 40 fulfilled prophecies to the 8, the chance would be 1 in 10 to the 157th power! That is 157 zeroes! Yet, all 61 prophecies were perfectly fulfilled just as God said they would be!

Jesus Christ is the absolute fulfillment of the Godhead as God foretold through the Scriptures. In addition to this, there is further confirmation of Jesus' resurrection as outlined in I Corinthians 15:1-8 where He appeared to more than 500 people after he was raised from the dead on the third day according to the Scriptures. The Bible is 100% correct according to what has been prophesied thus far. Even if you don't want to believe what is written in the Bible, there are historical accounts that run parallel with these recorded facts through the ages. There are maps that document where events occurred with names of ancient places from the Bible that were established as a result of what happened there. With so much that has been proven to be true, why would you even question what is left to be fulfilled. And that would be that Jesus is coming back, but this time, He's coming back to judge. Just read the book of Isaiah, written around 740 B.C., and you'll get a pretty good feel for how things are going to go down here. It's not pretty. Once He's here again, and we don't know when that will be, it will be too late for you to change your mind about who He is. As He told us when He was here before—only the Father knows the time of His return. When He came the first time, it was to save. Judgment will be his mission when He returns—my judgment and yours. Mercy from God is what we have right now, but justice is what is to come.

II.

The Relationship

Free Will

C. S. Lewis said it best, "There are 2 kinds of people: those who say to God "Thy will be done," and those to whom God says, "All right, then, have it your way."

Free will is a very controversial subject. Some believe that God predestined man to either believe in Him before the foundations of the earth or to not believe in Him before the foundations of the earth. I just don't see the point in that theory. I think we have a choice to make because to God, it's all about the relationship with Him. If you get nothing else out of reading the Bible, it's that. Otherwise, God, the Father, would have had no reason to send His Son to take on the Father's wrath for our sins. Where we go from here would have already been determined, but Jesus changed all of that. The two thieves that hung beside Him on the cross made that choice. One reviled Jesus, while the other, through his acceptance of who Jesus said He was, was told by Jesus that he would be with Him in Paradise.

The disciples represented free will in the truest sense. As Jesus' witnesses to His life and His teaching, they didn't expect Jesus to rise from the dead. Jesus had told them over and over again that He would die and three days later rise from the grave, but they did not understand Him. Jesus died, and these men were left with shattered hopes and dismal disappointment about His passing. But several days later, after the resurrection, these men were forever changed. Why—because they saw Him alive from the dead, as did more than 500 others. The disciples all went to their deaths proclaiming that Jesus was who He said He was. They chose to follow Him. Not because they were forced to. It would have been so much easier for them to deny Him and just go on with their lives, but they knew what was to come—their salvation through belief in

Him. This is what became of those who chose to follow Him: Andrew was crucified on a cross; Barnabas was stoned to death; Bartholemew was beaten, then crucified; James, half-brother of Jesus, was stoned to death; James the Less was thrown from a pinnacle of the temple and beaten to death; John was exiled to Patmos, but died later of old age in Ephesus; Jude was crucified; Matthew was speared to death; Luke was hanged from an olive tree; Mark was dragged through the streets by his feet and then burned to death; Peter was scourged and crucified upside down; Philip was crucified; Simon was crucified; Thomas was speared to death; Matthias was stoned to death; James, son of Zebedee, was killed by the sword (Foxe's Book of Martyrs by John Foxe).

As a young adult, nothing convinced me more absolutely of who Christ is than understanding the horrifying deaths of every disciple. They had no doubt about whom Jesus was, and everything He claimed to be because they witnessed it all with their own eyes.

Free will makes the choice a reality. God is challenging you to choose, and you have to take God on His terms, not yours. He makes certain that you can't choose to love Him unless you have the choice not to. This is the only way you are able to express genuine love for Him through the choice you make. That choice makes it clear to Him whether you want a relationship with Him or you don't. It's just that simple. You don't get to pick the moment you're born, and you don't get to choose the moment you die, but you do make the choices in between.

It certainly would have been easier for the disciples to lie to save themselves, but what they experienced wasn't a lie. It was the ultimate truth with serious consequences—no relationship with the God they knew and loved if they denied Him. Total separation. Again, it's all about the relationship.

The worst event in human history, Christ's crucifixion, ushered in the greatest circumstance in human history—salvation through Jesus Christ.

Unbelief

ou're not going to heaven because you think you are a good person either. Otherwise, Jesus' death on the cross would have been pointless. He hung on that cross and He took on all the wrath that God felt for us for our unbelief and our sins. All of that anger He put on His Son because Jesus was the only One who could bear it. He was the only perfect sacrifice—the only One who could satisfy God's plan to redeem us. Only then could we be saved, giving us everlasting life with Him who created us. You can't earn it through your good deeds because it is by the grace of God that you are saved, not by any moral standard. I don't want you to confuse salvation with morality, either. Moral and immoral people hung Jesus on the cross. Grace is giving you what you don't deserve. It levels the playing field for everyone. It's not about fairness or how good you think you are. It's given just because He loves us so much. Again, it's all about the relationship!

You are going to be asked to choose. Know this— you serve Satan if you reject Jesus Christ. You don't have to be a murderer or a thief either. All you have to do is ignore Jesus Christ. Jesus died on that cross to save you and me from sin and from hell. God is holy and will not allow sin to enter His kingdom. When you die in your sins, you are forever banished from the presence of God. And that will be hell. Your sins put you in hell, not God. "The Lord is not willing that any should perish, but that all should come to repentance" (II Peter 3:9).

There is a lengthy passage in Luke 16:19-31 told by Jesus about the rich man and the beggar, Lazarus. You should read it in its entirety, but I will include the very last part of the passage so that you get the picture. It will give you some fresh insight about unbelief and its consequences. Speaking from Hades regarding his brothers, the rich man says, "Father (Abraham) I beg you to send him (Lazarus) to my father's house—for I have five brothers—that he may warn them, so that they will not also come into this place of torment. Abraham replied, 'They have Moses and the prophets; they should listen to them.' He said, 'No, father Abraham; but if someone goes to them from the dead, they will repent.' Abraham said to him, 'If they do not listen to Moses and the prophets, neither will they be convinced even if someone rises from the dead.'"

Do not lose sight of the fact that even though we are all saved by grace if we choose to believe in Him, there will be judgment for all of us based on the way we lived our lives on this earth. Our deeds and an account of our lives will then be known to us through the Judge, Jesus Christ. You will see Him, face to face. *Will you be proud or ashamed to stand before Him?* It's your choice. If I were you, my greatest fear as I stood before Him in judgment would be to hear Him say, "I never knew you."

III.
The Pattern of Man

*I*t is such a good thing that everything we think as human beings is not revealed for others to see. We are basically different in reality from what we would want others to think of us. We all are born with this pattern of deceit that resides in our minds and hearts. It is inescapable as humans because it is part of our nature, our sinful nature.

Many people that I know believe Adam and Eve and the fall of man in the Garden of Eden is a myth, a fairy tale, a fable. This account of sin into human nature is scoffed and laughed at. Satan gets a pass as well.

God doesn't dismiss Satan so easily though, because He created him. He was an angelic being of the highest and most glorious kind. His name was Lucifer

(Isaiah 4:12). He was second only to God Himself, full of wisdom, brightness, and perfect beauty (Ezekiel 28:12-17). Lucifer had a very high opinion of himself and let pride get in the way of his judgment. *Who does that sound like?*

Angels, like us, possess free will. Lucifer wanted to be like God—to be worshiped and adored by the other angels that God created. Because of his prideful, rebellious nature Lucifer, was cast by God, out of heaven along with many other angels who chose to follow him. The Bible is not specific about when this event took place, but it was obviously before the creation of Adam and Eve. Satan wanted to be God. He thought He could be God, but only God can be God.

Earth now belongs to Satan—under his power and control. Satan exists in a spiritual realm as the deceiver of men, a lover of darkness.

This obviously runs contrary to the will of God for mankind. That's why God's plan for redemption is so crucial to you and to me. Satan and his minions will be defeated. Their doom is certain according to 1 John 3:8, "The Son of God was revealed for this purpose, to destroy the works of the devil."

IV.
The Sign of His Coming

The End of the Age

(Matthew 24:3-44) When He was sitting on the Mount of Olives, the disciples came to Him privately, saying, "Tell us, when will this be (the destruction of the Temple) and what will be the sign of Your coming and the end of the age?" Jesus answered them, "Beware that no one leads you astray. For many will come in My name, saying 'I am the Messiah!' and they will lead many astray. And you will hear of wars and rumors of wars; see that you are not alarmed; for this must take place, but the end is not yet. For nation will rise against nation, and kingdom against kingdom, and there will be famines and earthquakes in various places; all this is but the beginning of the birth pangs."

"Then they will hand you over to be tortured and will put you to death, and you will be hated by all nations because of My name. Then many will fall away, and they will betray one another. And many false prophets will arise and lead many astray."

"And because of the increase of lawlessness, the love of many will grow cold. But the one who endures to the end will be saved. And this good news of the kingdom will be proclaimed throughout the world, as a testimony to all the nations; and then the end will come."

"So, when you see the desolating sacrilege (the anti-Christ) standing in the holy place (the Temple), as was spoken of by the prophet Daniel (605 B.C.), then those in Judea (Israel) must flee to the mountains; the one on the housetop must not go down to take what is in the house; the one in the field must not turn back to get a coat."

"Woe to those who are pregnant and to those who are nursing infants in those days! Pray that your flight may not be in winter or on a Sabbath. For at that time there will be great suffering, such as has not been from the beginning of the world until now, no, and never will be."

"And if those days had not been cut short, no one would be saved; but for the sake of the elect (believers) those days will be cut short. Then if anyone says to you, 'Look! Here is the Messiah!' or 'There He is!'—do not believe it. For false messiahs and false prophets will appear and produce great signs and omens, to lead astray, if possible, even the elect. So, if they say to you, 'Look! He is in the wilderness,' do not go out. If they say, 'Look! He is in the inner rooms,' do not believe it. For as the lightning comes from the east and flashes as far as the west, so will be the coming of the Son of Man (Jesus Christ). Wherever the corpse is, there the vultures will gather."

"Immediately after the suffering of those days the sun will be darkened, and the moon will not give its light; the stars will fall from heaven, and the powers of heaven will be shaken."

"Then the sign of the Son of Man will appear in heaven, and then all the tribes of the earth will mourn, and they will see the Son of Man coming on the clouds of heaven with power and great glory. And he will send out his angels with a loud trumpet call, and they will gather his elect from the four winds, from one end of heaven to the other."

"From the fig tree learn its lesson: as soon as its branch becomes tender and puts forth its leaves, you know that summer is near. So also, when you see all these things, you know that He is near, at the very gates. Truly I tell you, this generation (of God's children, His spiritual offspring) will not pass away, until all these things have taken place. Heaven and earth will pass away, but my words will not pass away."

"But about that day and hour no one knows, neither the angels of heaven, nor the Son, but only the Father. For as the days of Noah were, so will be the coming of the Son of Man. For as in those days before the flood they were eating and drinking, marrying and giving in marriage, until the day Noah entered the ark, and they knew nothing until the flood came and swept them all away, so too will be the coming of the Son of Man. Then two will be in the field; one will be taken and one will be left. Two women will be grinding meal together; one will be taken and one will be left. Keep awake therefore, for you do not know on what day your Lord is coming. But understand this: if the owner of the house had known in what part of the night the thief was coming, he would have stayed awake and would not have let his house be broken into. Therefore you also must be ready, for the Son of Man is coming at an unexpected hour."

I had to quote the entire passage. It is just too important, especially considering that, it was all said by Jesus Christ, Himself.

Societal and Spiritual Decay

We live in a time when sheer annihilation of the planet by man is possible. No other armies in recent history can compare to the desolation that is now possible through nuclear and biological weapons. When Jesus was quoted above, evil weapons of mass destruction were obviously not a factor, but no nation can feel secure any longer. Violence, murder and lawlessness abound. In II Timothy 3:1-5, The Apostle Paul says, "You must understand this that in the last days distressing times will come. For people will be lovers of money, boasters, arrogant, abusive, disobedient to their parents, ungrateful, unholy, inhuman, implacable (unalterable), slanderers, profligates, brutes, haters of good, treacherous, reckless, swollen with deceit, lovers of pleasure rather than lovers of God, holding to the

outward form of godliness, but denying its power."
What do you think? Are we there yet? Every nation
throughout history that has descended to the lowest
depths of morality, as the United States seems to be
fast approaching, has ended.

Climate

You can talk all day about global warming or global cooling, or carbon footprints and climate change, but when it's all said and done, it is God who is in control. You can read all about it in the Book of Revelation.

Long before that book was written, He punished His own people (the Jews) with droughts and famine when their disobedience to Him became intolerable. What makes you think that won't happen to us in this day and time? Droughts, famine, earthquakes, and floods—they're all on the horizon for a people who think He won't stretch out His hand against them. Nothing you've ever seen can compare to what is coming. The Bible tells us so.

Persecution

Germany, prior to World War II, was the most cultured, educated nation on earth. By comparison to the rest of the world, Germany had the greatest number of people with masters and doctor's degrees of any other nation. What emerged from this nation was a man of unimaginable cruelty and evil. I'm sure most people eventually came to believe that Hitler was the anti-Christ, having exterminated more than 6 million Jews. He certainly lived up to the reputation as one of them, but there is a far worse force on the horizon than Hitler could ever be compared to. This degree of evil is unparalleled in history, and he plans to raise an army of followers that will engage in the persecution of the entire planet. "For our struggle is not against enemies of flesh and blood, but against the rulers, against the authorities, against the cosmic powers of this present darkness, against the spiritual forces of evil in the heavenly places" (Ephesians 6:12).

Financial Crisis

As I write this book, the United States government is engaged in the largest monetary power grab in recorded history. It is a suspicious situation that came upon us as a nation with such urgency and haste that making sense of it is difficult. Those primarily responsible for oversight, or in this case, the lack of oversight regarding the sub-prime lending practices which eventually poisoned many financial institutions on Wall Street, are the very ones who will oversee the so-called solution to the problem and it's implementation—the U.S. Congress. What Osama Bin Laden couldn't destroy in New York City, Washington D.C., and Pennsylvania with airplanes—collapsing our entire financial system—our government seems to be able to destroy quite handily without too much opposition from the citizenry, who will be saddled with a debt of unimaginable proportions.

The mainstream media has been complicit with much of the unrest we see at this time in our financial markets. They beat the drum daily about how hopeless the future is.

What does this have to do with *the end of the age*? A lot. Nowhere in the Bible is there any mention of America, much less the United States. Could that be because throughout the Scriptures we are lumped in with all the nations of the world as a global entity? Possibly, after all the U.S. is just a blip on the radar screen in the timeline of world history. We've been around as a presence for only a few hundred years, compared to the Middle East, Europe and Asia that have been evident since history was first recorded and represent a large presence in Biblical prophecy.

The other answer to the question above could be that we may suddenly cease to exist as a world power or even exist, period. As a world power, the debt that we are accumulating is so enormous that a viable solution to save us financially seems unattainable. The result could be a world monetary system that is alluded to in the book of Revelation 13:16-18, "It causes all, both small and great, both rich and poor, both free and slave, to be marked on the right hand or forehead, so that no one can buy or sell who does not have the mark, that is, the name of the beast (false prophet) or the number of its name. This calls for wisdom; let anyone with understanding calculate the number of the beast, for it is the number of a person. Its number is six hundred sixty-six" (Hebrew and Greek letters have numerical equivalents, the number of the beast (666) is the sum of the separate letters of his name, the false prophet). Just remember that whoever controls the money rules the world. The quest for world domination is undoubtedly connected through the exchange of money.

I have touched on a few of the signs that should throw up some big, red flags. It is not my intention to scare you to death, but it is my intention to make you see the "handwriting on the wall". By the way, that phrase can be found in Daniel 5: 5-7. It is obvious as I write this book that evil and corruption are increasing at a very fast pace as the Bible said it would as we draw nearer to the *end of the age.*

V.

Where Will You Turn?

So, the fulfillment of future prophecy in the Bible seems to indicate a great tribulation unlike anything the earth and its inhabitants have ever seen or experienced. Believers in the Lord, Jesus Christ have some assurance that they will not have to endure most of this period as I previously stated in Matthew 24. Verse 22 declares in Jesus' own words, "If those days had not been cut short, no one would be saved; but for the sake of the elect (believers) those days will be cut short."

Where will these believers go? We are told by the apostle, Paul, in I Thessalonians 4:15-17 "We (believers) who are alive, who are left until the coming of the Lord, will by no means precede those who have died. For the Lord Himself, with a cry of command with the archangel's call and with the sound of God's trumpet, will descend from heaven, and the dead in Christ will rise first. Then we who are alive, who are left, will be caught up in the clouds together with them to meet the Lord in the air (the rapture), and so we will be with the Lord forever. Therefore encourage one another with these words." I Thessalonians 5:1-2 further clarifies, "Concerning the times and seasons, brothers and sisters, you do not need to have anything written to you. For you yourselves know very well that the day of the Lord will come like a thief in the night." I Corinthians 15:50-52 paints an even clearer picture, "Flesh and blood cannot inherit the kingdom of God, nor does the imperishable. Listen, I will tell you a mystery! We will not all die, but we will all be changed, in a moment, in the twinkling of an eye, at the last trumpet." These people will vanish from the face of the earth. *What do you think you will do when that happens? Where will you turn? Will you think that they were taken away by aliens?* I am sure that will be one explanation. Maybe you'll remember what you read in this book. It won't be too late because Christ has not physically returned to earth for the purpose of judgment. Please, if you're still here, still alive at this time, reconsider which path to choose. There is time.

I have no idea how long a period it will be between the rapture of believers and the horrifying destruction of this earth, but understand that what is here now will be totally destroyed. John says so with great clarity in the book of Revelation because Jesus plans to "create a new heaven and a new earth." "The home of God is among mortals. He will dwell with them as their God." Chapter 21 goes into serious detail about how He will make all things new. "Death will be no more."

There is so much to learn about who God is. He created you to worship Him, not the other way around. Turning to Him is the only way to secure your future, your salvation. All the glory goes to Him! You must see that by now. Jesus said in John 14:13, "I will do whatever you ask in My name, so that the Father may be glorified in the Son." People are saved from their sins to give God the glory that He deserves. To turn away from Him is the gravest insult you can ever imagine. He has given you all this time to figure this out, so don't miss it! That's why you're here on this planet! There are many passages that explain the alternative. The main thing you need to know is that the alternative will be total separation from Him. You won't get another chance according to everything that I have ever read and believe me in all sincerity, I've looked for other explanations. There are none. On that subject, Jesus is very, very clear. "I am the way, the truth, and the life. No one comes to the Father except through Me. If you know Me, you will know My Father also. From now on you do know Him and have seen Him" (John 14:6-7).

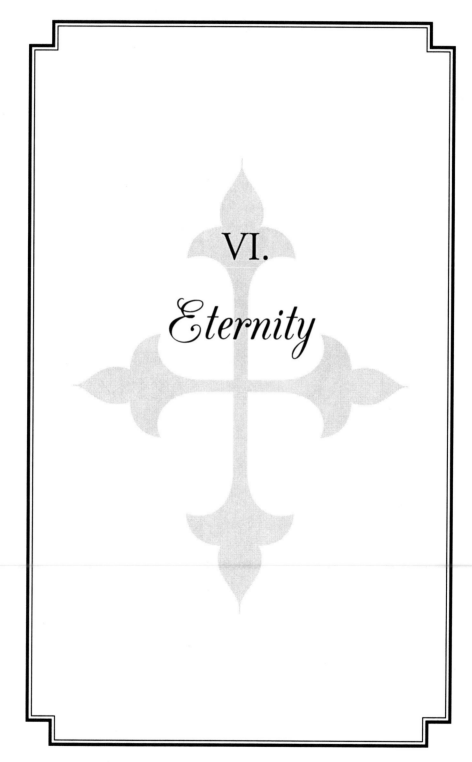

VI.

Eternity

*I*t is not timeless, but endless. If God is eternal, time must be infinite as well. Think about that for a moment. I think the safe thing to say is that eternity is forever, and it is a mystery how God coexists with the world.

Everybody wants to go to heaven, don't they? Ask yourself this question. Is the God you've ignored, denied, or even hated burning a place in your heart now for all eternity? You don't want to die without Christ. I can find no place in the Bible that gives you any other option but Him. Don't put your faith in mankind, either, because as God said through Isaiah in the book of Isaiah 2:17-22, "The pride of man will be humbled and the loftiness of men will be abased (humiliated, degraded); and the Lord alone will be exalted in that day, but the idols will completely vanish. Men will go into caves of the rocks and into holes of the ground before the terror of the Lord and the splendor of His majesty, when He arises to make the earth tremble. In that day men will hide to the moles and bats, their idols of silver and their idols of gold, which they made for themselves to worship, in order to go into the caverns of the rocks and the clefts of the cliffs before the terror of the Lord and the splendor of His majesty, when he arises to make the earth tremble. Stop regarding man, whose breath of life is in his nostrils; for why should he be esteemed?" The things of this world, man included, are passing away.

Christ has to mean everything to you. The evidence of your faith in Him is a changed life, an ongoing process of refinement. You must experience a conversion of your heart in order to have eternal life with Him. You have to want this more than anything you've ever desired. He expects nothing less. It is going to cost you, though—because the world will hate you.

"If the world hates you, be aware that it hated Me (Jesus) before it hated you. If you belonged to the world, the world would love you as its own. Because you do not belong to the world, but I have chosen you out of the world—therefore the world hates you" (John 15:18). "Whoever hates Me hates My Father also" (John 15:23). "I have said this to you, so that in Me you may have peace. In the world you face persecution. But take courage; I have conquered the world" (John 16:33)!

Praying for His Spirit to come into your life is the first step to knowing Him, but you are going to have to believe in the truth of the Gospel of Jesus Christ to be considered a follower of His and to receive the gift of eternal life. *Are you prepared to do that?*

I don't know if this book has made any difference in what you believe or don't believe, but I do know that God is waiting for you and beside yourself, He is the only one who truly knows what is in your heart. Wherever you are in your life, whatever you may think is unforgivable—God will listen if you repent.

Just don't make the mistake of thinking that you are blameless of sin in this life, that you are your own god. Pride has been a stumbling block for many—don't let it trip you up. My own life is a "work in progress" with a sinful nature at my core. I recognize my shortcomings—pride, hypocrisy, immoral behavior, irreverence, idolizing things and people instead of Him, cursing, gossiping, you name it—I've probably done it and there have been consequences for my behavior. I am a different person having had Him in my life than I would have ever been without Him. It is only through the Lord, Jesus Christ that I can live day to day with any hope for salvation. He is the perfection that I default to because I cannot claim any form of perfection for myself. He chose to give you and me this gift of everlasting life—we have to choose to receive it. *Will You?*

Eternity is endless. In fact, we can't even wrap our arms around the concept of it because our lives on earth are arranged around finite circumstances in time.

God exchanged Jesus for you and for me when He hung on the cross. That was the primary component of His plan for redemption that we include as part of the Gospel of Jesus Christ. If you miss that—you'll miss it all. "God so loved the world that He gave His only Son, so that everyone who believes in Him may not perish but may have eternal life" (John 3:16). "Those who believe in Me, even though they die, will live, and everyone who lives and believes in me will never die" (John 11:25-26). He loves us beyond our level of understanding. And why in the world should He? We don't deserve His love. Most humans don't even want to admit that He even exists. Fortunately for all of us, He is as fair a judge, as we will ever know. In my own mind and heart, through what He has revealed to me, our existence on this earth is all about choosing Him or not choosing Him. He's given us just enough information to make that choice—He is the hope and truth of the life to come. No, we don't have all of the answers, but He does.

"If you indeed cry out for insight, and raise your voice for understanding; if you seek it like silver, and search for it as for hidden treasures—then you will understand the fear of the Lord and find the knowledge of God" (Proverbs 2: 3-5).

I leave you with this, a line spoken from a pastor sometime ago, who through many years of prophetic research, hoping to unravel the mysteries of the Bible, came to this simple conclusion:

"HE'S COMING, WE DON'T KNOW WHEN, AND WE BETTER BE READY!"

Journal

Suggested Reading and Viewing

The Bible

The Case for the Real Jesus, Book by Lee Strobel

The Case for Faith, DVD by Lee Strobel, Narrated by
    Ed Ragozzino of Eugene, Oregon

Indescribable, DVD by Louie Giglio

How Great is Our God, DVD by Louie Giglio

About the Author

Stacie Shukanes is an Interior Designer by education and profession. It has been a satisfying career, but it was never the fulfillment of her life. When her daughter was very young, she began a Bible study that started her on a journey to find out the purpose of her existence on this earth. She has seen that journey crescendo through the years, coloring her life with a richness of faith that comes only from an indepth study of the Bible. This book, *The Exchange, Him for You*, is a culmination of information, purposely put in a brief format, that Stacie has collected to convey God's message about the life to come to everyone in her circle of family and friends who could miss this opportunity. There are choices to make about this life that transcend to the next. There is an eternity and where you spend it is the foundational premise of the book.

There have been many reasons to write this book, but the most important one for Stacie is to spread the Gospel of Jesus Christ in a way that is easy to understand and not laden with complex theories and page upon page of tedious Scripture.

Stacie is also a Precept Upon Precept leader at First Baptist Church of Eugene, Oregon, and she participates in two other local studies of the Bible with her many Christian friends.

Printed in the United States
130726LV00002B/41/P

9 781438 928821